GRUMPY CAT's
MISERABLE
PAPERCRAFT BOOK

Jimi Bonogofsky-Gronseth

Dover Publications, Inc
Mineola, New York

Bibliographical Note

Grumpy Cat's Miserable Papercraft Book is a new work, first
published by Dover Publications, Inc, in 2015

International Standard Book Number

ISBN-13: 978-0-486-80321-0
ISBN-10: 0-486-80321-X

Manufactured in the United States by RR Donnelley
80321X01   2015
wwwdoverpublicationscom

Contents

GRUMPY CAT DOESN'T LIKE BOWS

SCISSORS · TAPE OR GLUE
(optional) Bobby pin, hair clip, or ribbon

YOU DID THIS TO ME.

YOU MONSTER.

1. Bend the edges of shape A back until they meet in the center. Th will create a bow shape; press lightly on the bow to flatten it slightly, but do not crease.

2. Place bow onto shape B; this wil form the tails of the bow. Tape o glue the two shapes together.

3. Wrap shape C around the center of both and tape closed.

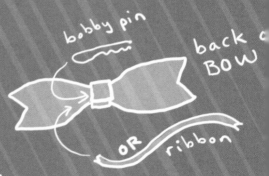

bobby pin

back o BOW

OR ribbon

4. For a hair clip, slide a bobby pin through the back of the center piece, or glue to a hair clip. For a bow tie, slide a ribbon through th back of the center piece.

make it a
hideous hair bow

or a ridiculous
bow tie

either way,
you'll look awful.

A.

B.

C.

← cut these
out.

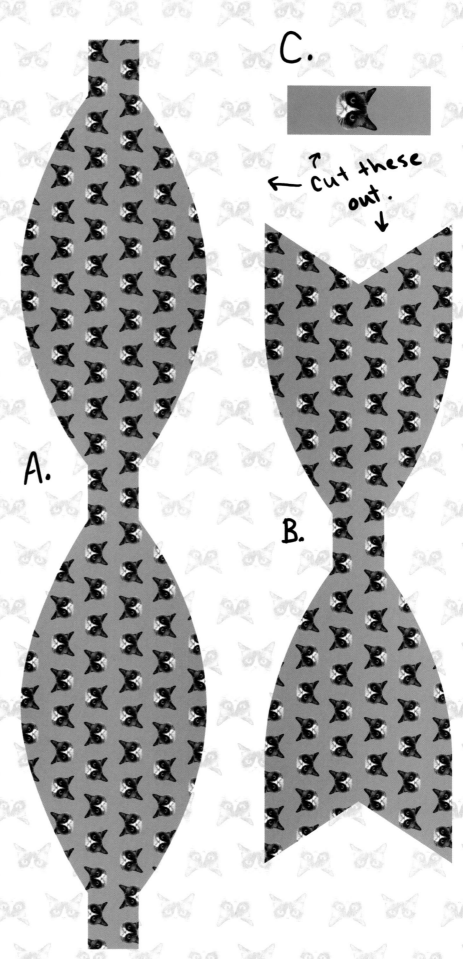

5

GRUMPY CAT DOESN'T LIKE DICE

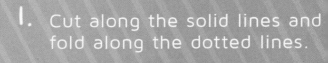

SCISSORS • GLUE

1. Cut along the solid lines and fold along the dotted lines.

2. Glue the white tabs beneath the corresponding edge.

3. Roll away!

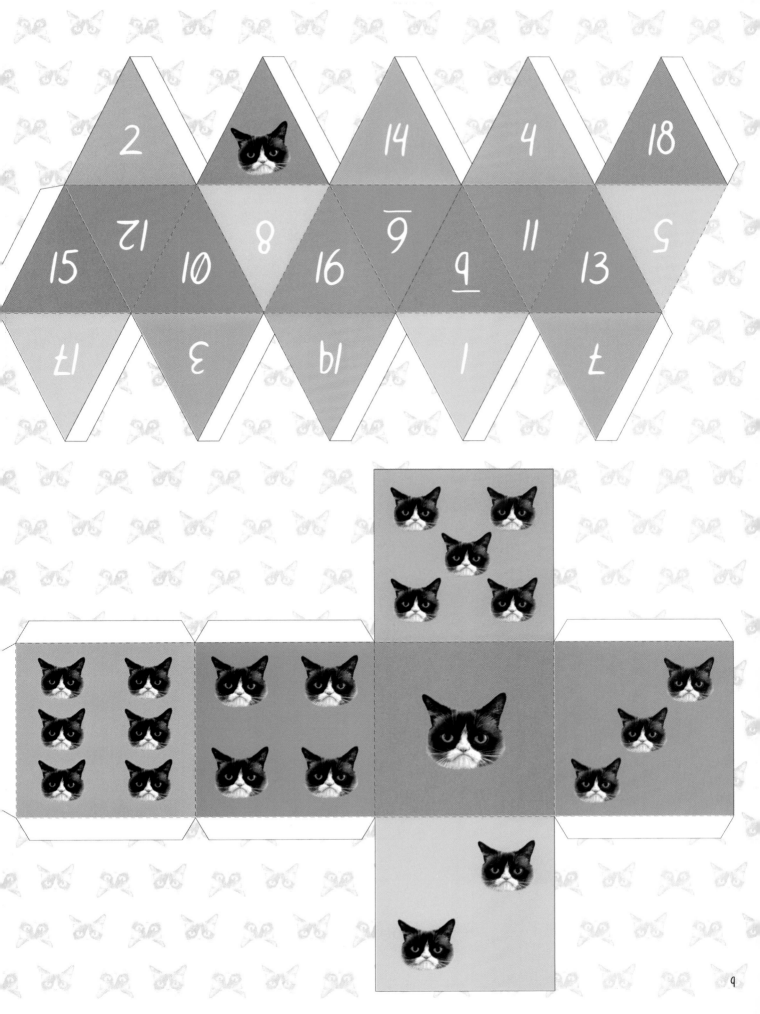

9

GRUMPY CAT DOESN'T LIKE | DOORKNOB HANGERS

SCISSORS

Cut along the white line and cut out the white circle on each doorknob hanger.

GRUMPY CAT DOESN'T LIKE FINGER PUPPETS

CRAFT KNIFE · GLUE

1. Cut out the shapes to the left.

2. Fold in half.

3. Apply a thin layer of glue to each coloured tab, then glue to the inside of the corresponding side.

4. Place on finger and put on a grumpy show!

UGH...

I HOPE YOU GET A PAPERCUT WHEN YOU WEAR IT.

13

GRUMPY CAT DOESN'T LIKE | FLOWER ORNAMENTS

SCISSORS · TAPE · STRING

1. Cut out all the flowers and along the white lines on each flower.

2. Poke a hole into the purple flower with the white dot using the tip of your scissors. Thread each end of a 5" string through the hole to form a loop for the ornament hanger. Tape the ends to the bottom of the flower shape to secure it.

3. Connect the flowers together by sliding each petal into the other.

4. Continue until you have a full flower made of frowns.

ONCE, I STOPPED TO SMELL THE ROSES. IT WAS AWFUL.

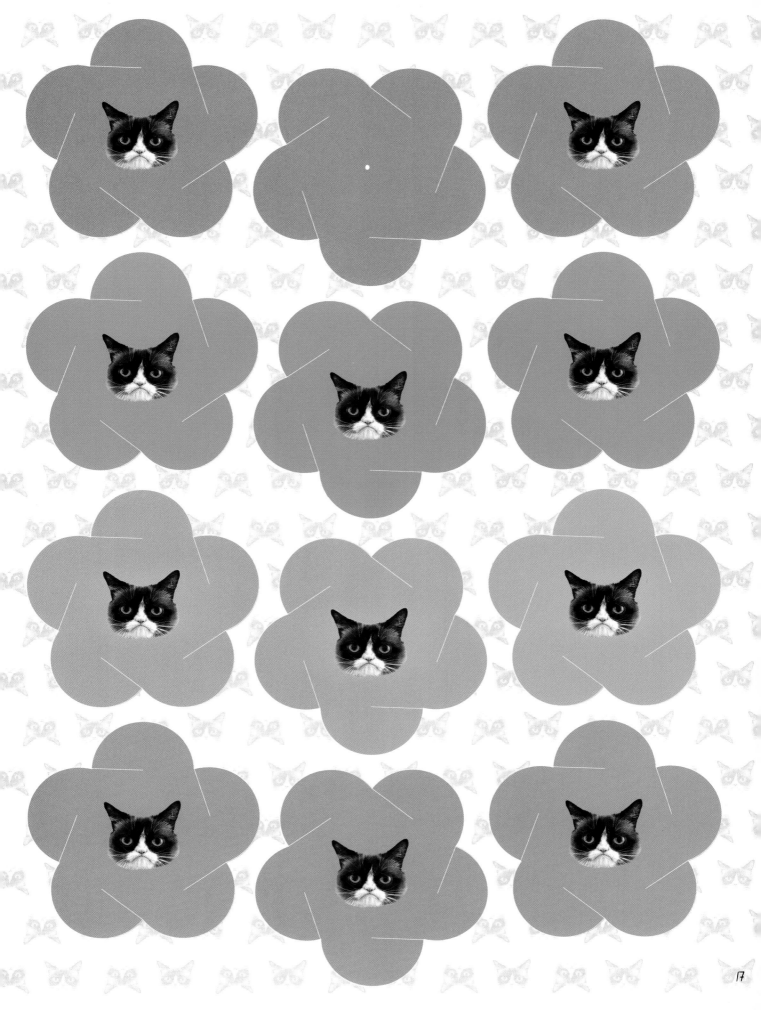

GRUMPY CAT DOESN'T LIKE | FORTUNE COOKIES

SCISSORS · TAPE

1. Fold in half without creasing, design side out.

crease

2. Crease ONLY the middle third, then unfold.

3. Fold in half the opposite way, without creasing.

4. Slide the fortune inside the "cookie."

Gently press the crease inward, allowing the edges of the paper to roll together slightly.

tape

Fold the ends in until they meet, securing them with a small roll of tape between

MY FORTUNES ARE SUPER ACCURATE. ENJOY.

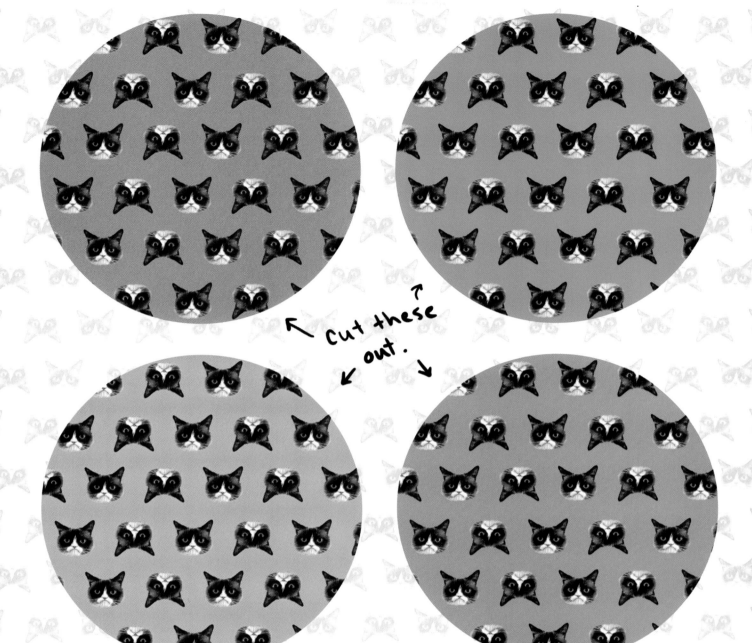

cut these out.

Next Tuesday, you'll realize that your entire existence is pointless.

Every risk you take this month will fail. So, you know. Go for it.

Don't bother being the change you want to see in the world. No one listens to you, anyhow.

Opportunity is knocking at your door. Wait. Nope. It had the wrong address. Too bad.

Favor the color blue today. It will help guide you into further sadness and despair.

Apathy is easier. Embrace it.

Fortune and great wealth will be yours next week. Hahahahahaha. I have the best jokes.

Right now, someone is thinking about you. And laughing.

GRUMPY CAT DOESN'T LIKE | FORTUNES

1. With the printed side on the back, fold in half horizontally, then unfold. Repeat vertically and diagonally.

2. Fold each corner to the center of the page.

3. Flip.

4. Repeat step 3.

5. Flip.

6. It should look like this.

YOU WANT ME TO TELL YOU YOUR FORTUNE?

IT'LL JUST BE DISAPPOINTING.

7. Fold in half vertically, unfold.

8. Fold in half horizontally.

9. Place your thumbs and index fingers in each of the four pockets.

IT'LL LOOK LIKE THIS.

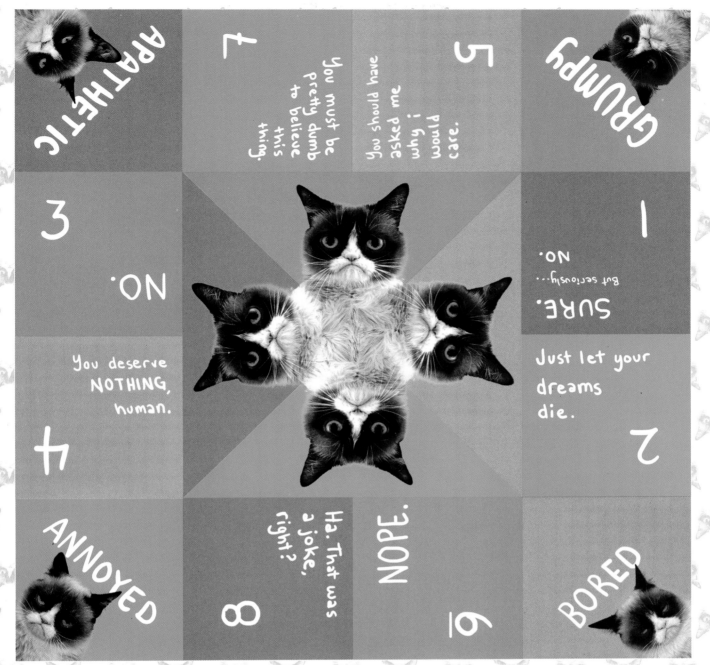

cut out.

HOW TO PLAY

1. Put each thumb and index finger in one of the four pockets of the device.

2. Have a friend ask Grumpy Cat one yes or no question.

3. Have your friend choose one of the emotions on the device.

4. Spell out the emotion, and with each letter alternate pinching the device in and pulling it out to display all the odd numbers, then all the even numbers.

5. Once you've spelled the word, stop. Have your friend pick a number from one of the four visible.

6. Repeat step 5, this time counting with the number your friend picked.

7. Once you have reached their number, have them pick another number from those displayed. Fold back the flap of that number to reveal the fortune hiding beneath!

GRUMPY CAT DOESN'T LIKE GARLAND

SCISSORS · TAPE · STRING

1. Carefuly cut out each shape.

2. Bend each tab back at the dotted line.

3. Tape the tab closed on the back.

4. Slide each shape onto a string or ribbon; the length is up to you.

5. If you are draping the garland instead of tying it taut, consider taping the string to the inside of the tab loop.

6. Worst. Party. Ever.

YES, I HAVE STRING FOR YOUR GARLAND.

NO, YOU CAN'T HAVE ANY OF IT.

NOPE NOPE NOPE NOPE NOPE

GIFT BOXES

CRAFT KNIFE • GLUE

1. Carefully cut out the gift box.

2. Using a craft knife, cut around Grumpy's ears.

3. Fold along each dark line, being careful NOT to fold Grumpy's ears down.

4. Apply a thin layer of glue to each numbered tab and glue beneath its corresponding side.

5. Put something in the box, close the lid, and you now have a lovely (albeit grumpy) gift box!

I'LL BET MY BOX IS BETTER THAN YOUR GIFT.

GRUMPY CAT DOESN'T LIKE HEARTS

SCISSORS · GLUE

1. Cut along all the solid black lines, including down towards the center of the heart.

2. Apply a thin layer of glue along one side of the center slit on the design side.

3. Press the two sides of the slit together. This will make the center of the heart pop out. Hold til dry.

WAYS TO USE THE STUPID HEARTS

Use sticky tack to make a heart mural.

Glue onto a card or wrapped present.

Glue hearts along string for garland.

WHY IS MY FACE ON SO MANY HEARTS?

STOP.
STOP IT NOW.

GRUMPY CAT DOESN'T LIKE HEX GIFT BOXES

SCISSORS • TAPE OR GLUE

1. Carefully cut out the shape to the right.

2. Fold each of the arms up at the edges of the hexagon.

3. Crease each arm inwards along the dotted lines.

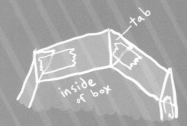

4. Tape or glue each triangle shape to the inside of the rectangle shape next to it to form the box sides.

5. Put something in the box. Preferably something your friend will not like.

6. Interlock the arms by wrapping the arm on the left beneath the one on the right, then sliping the circled end on top. Continue till the box is closed.

YOUR BOX IS STUPID. MINE IS STUPENDOUS.

GRUMPY CAT DOESN'T LIKE MASKS

SCISSORS • STRING OR ELASTIC

1. Cut out the mask, including the eye holes.
2. Make slits at the white lines on either side.
3. Attach string or elastic.
4. Wear proudly.

GRUMPY CAT DOESN'T LIKE | COFFEE SLEEVES

SCISSORS · GLUE

glue here

1. Cut out the coffee cup sleeve below.

2. Apply a thin layer of glue on the left side as indicated and glue to the back of the right side. Let dry.

3. Slide onto your coffee cup. Don't spill.

COFFEE IS THE ONLY REASON I'M TOLERATING YOU RIGHT NOW.

YOU THINK I'M GRUMPY NOW? TRY ME BEFORE MY MORNING COFFEE.

MEMORY CARDS

SCISSORS

CUT OUT THE CARDS FIRST.

HOW TO PLAY
(2+ players)

1. Shuffle cards and lay them out in a grid, backs facing up.

2. Decide who goes first, then the first player turns over two cards. If they match, keep the pair and go again. In the more likely scenario that they don't match, end your turn.

3. Flip the cards back over, but don't relocate them.

4. Continue until all matches have been found. Whoever has the most matches doesn't lose.

HOW TO PLAY
(1 player variant)

Keep track of how many turns it takes you to match the cards. This is not recommended as a Tarot deck.

THERE ARE NO WINNERS.

ONLY SECOND-PLACE LOSERS.

GRUMPY CAT
DISLIKES
MEMORY
CARDS

GRUMPY CAT
DISLIKES
MEMORY
CARDS

GRUMPY CAT
DISLIKES
MEMORY
CARDS

GRUMPY CAT
DISLIKES
MEMORY
CARDS

GRUMPY CAT
DISLIKES
MEMORY
CARDS

GRUMPY CAT
DISLIKES
MEMORY
CARDS

GRUMPY CAT
DISLIKES
MEMORY
CARDS

GRUMPY CAT
DISLIKES
MEMORY
CARDS

GRUMPY CAT
DISLIKES
MEMORY
CARDS

GRUMPY CAT
DISLIKES
MEMORY
CARDS

GRUMPY CAT
DISLIKES
MEMORY
CARDS

GRUMPY CAT
DISLIKES
MEMORY
CARDS

GRUMPY CAT DOESN'T LIKE | MOBILES

SCISSORS · TAPE · STRING

1. Cut out the strips. Starting at the starred end, design side up, fold back along the dotted lines, alternating folds back and forth like an accordian.

2. Once you reach the end, unfold everything, then reverse all of the straight folds. Unfold again.

3. Starting with the starred end, bend the strip so the single-starred edge meets the double-starred edge. This will create four sides of a six-sided, 3D shape.

4. Continue wrapping the paper beneath to complete the six-sided shape.

5. The paper will want to naturally wrap around this six-sided shape. Continue until you reach the end.

6. Tuck the final end into the fold beneath it.

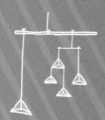

7. Knot the end of a string, then tape inside the fold at the top of each shape. Hang in a doorway or attach to a stick.

THIS ISN'T REALLY MY IDEA OF "HANGING OUT."

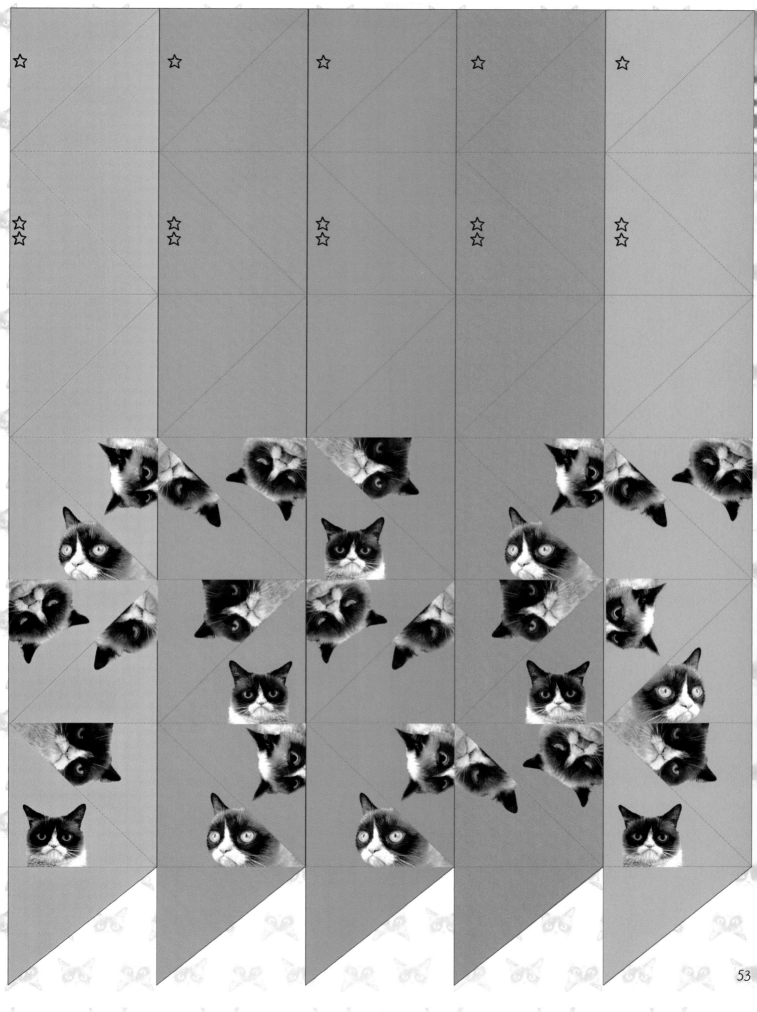

SCISSORS

1. Fold diagonally, design side out, with Grumpy Cat at the lower right.

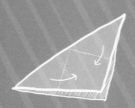

2. Fold left and right corners to bottom corner.

3. Fold same corners up at the angle shown.

4. Fold left and right corners in.

5. Fold top corner down.

6. Fold the bottom corner up.

7. Flip.

8. Ta-da. Great job.

YOU LIKE ORIGAMI? WOW... YOU MUST HAVE A LOT OF TIME ON YOUR HANDS.

CAREFULLY CUT OUT

CAREFULLY CUT OUT

GRUMPY CAT DOESN'T LIKE | PAPER BEADS

SCISSORS • GLUE • TOOTHPICKS • CLEAR NAIL POLISH

↖ glue

1. Carefully cut out the strips.

2. Apply a thin layer of glue on the back of the strip, starting a half inch from the wide end.

3. Tightly wrap the paper around the toothpick, starting at the wide end. Hold in place until dry.

CLEAR NAIL POLISH

4. Seal the bead with clear nail polish. Let dry.

5. Now go make something grumpy!

YOUR FASHION SENSE IS TERRIBLE.

GRUMPY CAT DOESN'T LIKE PAPER CHAINS

CUT OUT EACH SHAPE, THEN TAPE THE ENDS TOGETHER.

I HOPE THESE CHAINS IMPRISON YOUR HAPPINESS.

STOP TRYING

NO

NOT IMPRESSED

NOPE

GRUMPY CAT DOESN'T LIKE | PAPER ROCKETS

SCISSORS · GLUE · TAPE · PENCIL · STRAW

1. Cut out all four shapes.

glue

2. Apply a thin layer of glue to the back of one of the long sides.

3. Starting with the un-glued long side, wrap around a pencil. Hold till dry.

←tape

4. Slide one of the ends off the paper slightly, then tape it closed.

5. Remove from the pencil entirely and slide onto a straw.

6. Battle your friends for honor and glory.

YES...

EMBRACE YOUR INNER GRUMPINESS AS YOU BATTLE YOUR FRIENDS WITH STUPID TOYS.

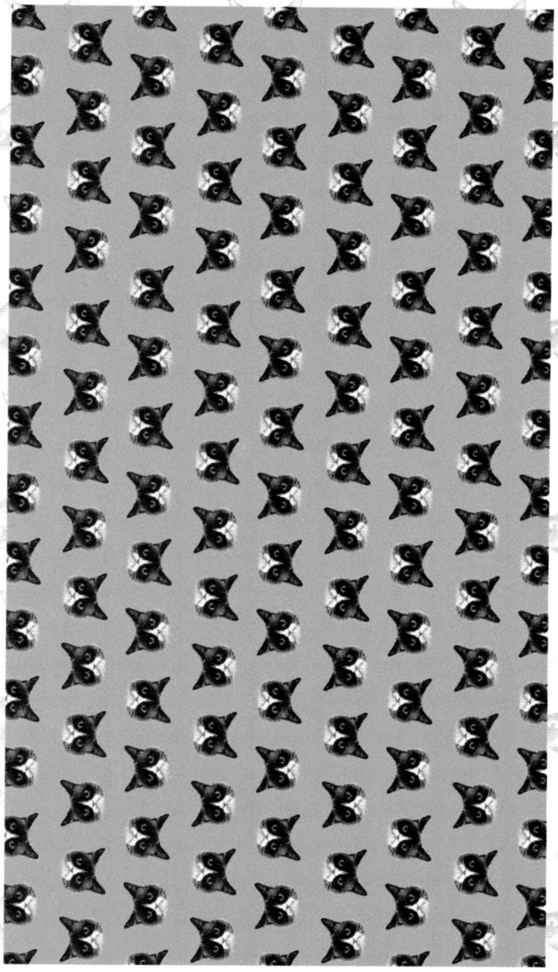

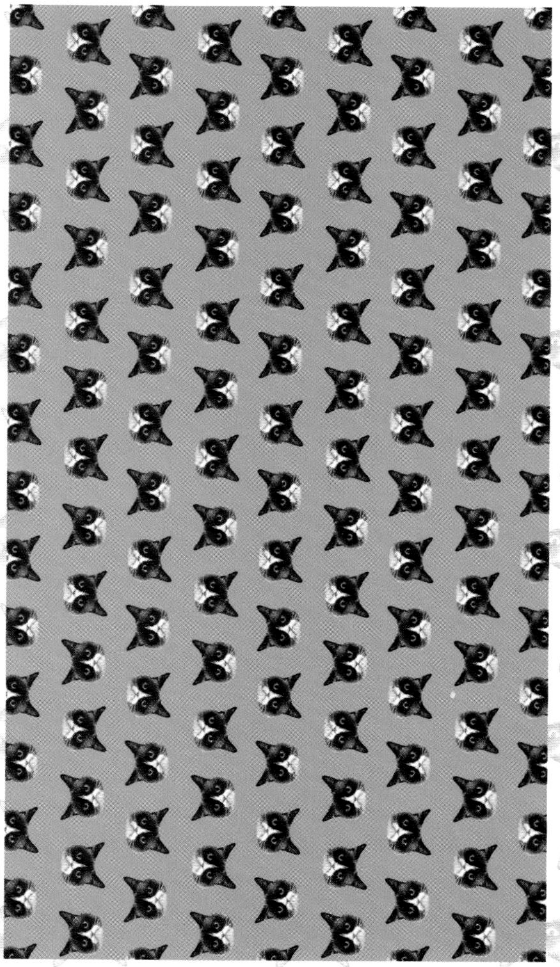

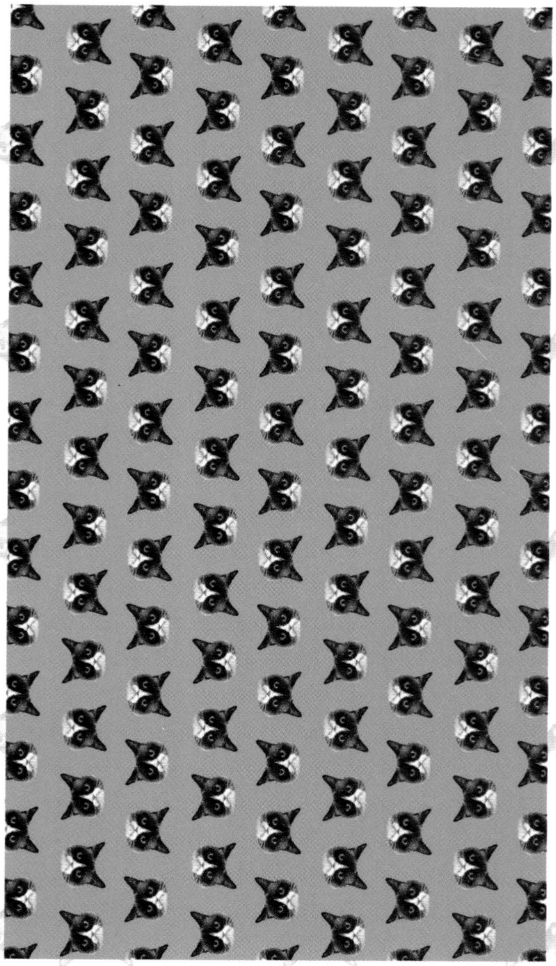

GRUMPY CAT DOESN'T LIKE | PAPER FOOTBALL

SCISSORS

1. Cut out the orange strip to the left. Turn the paper over so the design side is facing down.

2. Starting at the corner marked with a star, fold at the dotted line, and continue folding until you reach the rectangle block beneath Grumpy.

3. Fold down the corner beneath Grumpy along the dotted line and tuck into the pocket of the triangle.

HOW TO PLAY

1. On a table with a staight edge, take turns flicking the Grumpy Football. Your goal is to get it as close to the edge as possible. If it hangs off the edge without falling, you get a TOUCHDOWN (one point). If it falls over the edge, your turn is over.

2. If you get a touchdown, you can try for a field goal. Have your friend form goal posts with index fingers and thumbs, stand the Grumpy Football up, and try to flick it through the goal posts for another point.

3. Decide how many points it takes to win. Best out of 47?

DON'T YOU DARE FLICK ME.

GRUMPY CAT DOESN'T LIKE PARTY HATS

SCISSORS · TAPE · STRING

WHY MAKE A PARTY HAT WHEN NO ONE INVITES YOU TO PARTIES?

1. Cut out the hat below.

2. Roll the hat into a cone and tape the blue tab beneath the opposing side.

3. Tape two strands of string on the inside of each side of the hat.

4. Tie the string strands together beneath your chin.

5. Have a grumpy party!

PARTY ANIMAL

GRUMPY CAT DOESN'T LIKE PINWHEELS

SCISSORS · BALL HEAD PIN · NEW PENCIL

1. Cut out the pinwheel, including along the white lines at each corner. Flip the paper over so the design is facing down.

2. Take one corner (with Grumpy Cat on the back of it) and bend towards the center, holding it in place so the dot on Grunpy's chest lines up with the dot in the middle of the page.

3. Repeat this with each corner that has Grumpy on the back, holding the corners in place.

4. Push the pin through the dots to affix the corners to the middle of the page.

pin
pinwheel

5. Using a pair of needle nose pliers, carefully bend the needle at a 90 degree angle. Push the pin into the eraser of a new pencil.

6. Now blow your stupid little pinwheel like a child.

GRUMPY CAT DOESN'T LIKE LOVE CARDS

SCISSORS • CRAFT KNIFE • GLUE OR TAPE

1. Cut out both shapes to the right; the blue is the outside of the card, the pink is the inside of it.

2. Using a craft knife, cut along the white lines on the pink piece. Do NOT cut along the dark pink lines. Those are fold lines.

3. Gently fold the top four dark pink lines

4. Slowly begin to fold the entire thing in half, design facing in; the heart should begin to push out slightly. Complete the fold and press down to crease.

5. Fold the blue piece in half now, design facing out.

6. Tape or glue the two pieces together, the pink one inside the blu one. Be sure to apply adhesives around the heart shape, not inside otherwise it won't pop up when opened.

JUST FOR THE RECORD... I WOULD NEVER SEND YOU ONE OF THESE.

I DON'T COMPLETELY HATE YOU.
I GUESS.

I HOLD THESE FEELINGS I NEED TO CONFESS...

POP-UP CARDS

SCISSORS • CRAFT KNIFE • TAPE OR GLUE

1. Cut out the shapes to the right and Grumpy's face below. Slice along the solid lines in the middle of the inside of the card.

2. Fold the inside card in half, design facing in, then open. Reverse the fold of the center sliced portion so it folds inside of the card.

3. Glue the Grumpy Cat head to the base of the square pop-out.

4. Fold the orange, outer card in half, design facing out.

glue or tape

5. Apply glue or tape to the back of the purple card (NOT on the pop-out portion) and put inside the orange card.

6. Write some grump one-liners in the chat bubbles.

GREETING CARDS? I PREFER "LEAVE ME ALONE" CARDS.

CUT ME OUT

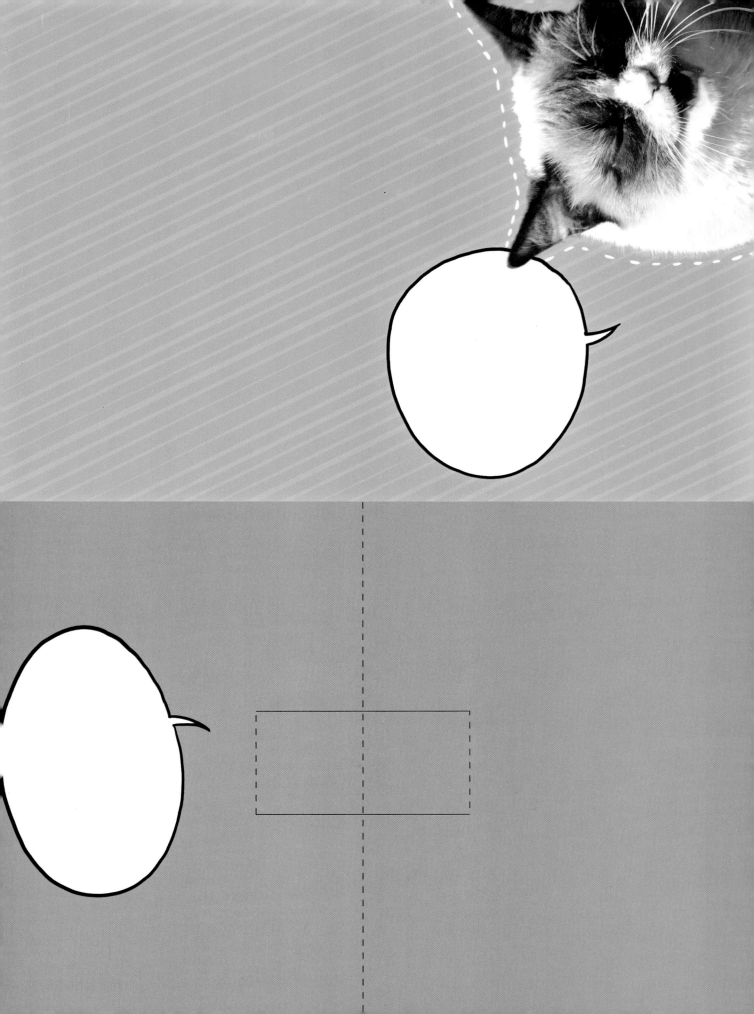

SPINNERS

SCISSORS · PAPER CLIPS

1. Cut out each individual square. Design side down, fold a square in half horizontally, then vertically.

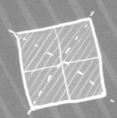

2. Flip over, then fold in half diagonally, in both directions.

3. Flip over again and push in on each side to fold inwards; this will create a triangle shape.

top. view

4. Each piece has two white corners. Slide the white corners of one piece into the solid coloured corners of another.

5. Secure with a paperclip.

6. Continue this process until you have connected all six pieces. No white corners should be showing.

7. Hold between your thumb and index finger and blow to make it spin.

I'M BLOWN AWAY. REALLY.

GRUMPY CAT DOESN'T LIKE | 3D PAPER FIGURES

CRAFT KNIFE • GLUE

1. Cut out the three shapes. Bold lines indicate where to cut, dotted lines indicate where to fold.

2. Glue the tabs beneath their corresponding edge.

3. Glue the bottom of the head to the top of the body.

D

A

A

C

C

B

D

YOU ARE MAKING A MOCKERY OF MY GLORIOUS FORM.

BODY

96

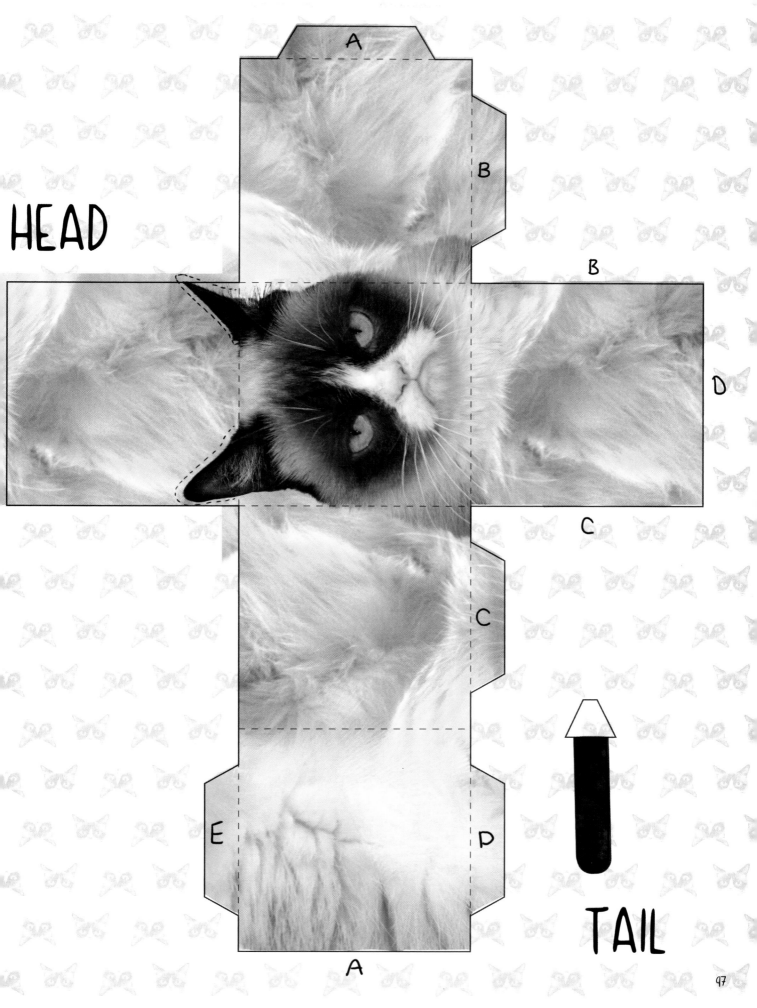

HEAD

A

B

B

D

C

C

D

E

F

A

TAIL

97

GRUMPY CAT DOESN'T LIKE | ORIGAMI STARS

It takes a little practice to get these stars to take shape. You might want to practice on spare strips of paper first.

SCISSORS

1. Carefully cut out the long strips.

2. Gently tie a knot at the end of one strip, allowing about a quarter inch tab. This will form a pentagon.

3. Flip over and tuck the tab into the fold.

4. Wrap the long strip over the pentagon. Continue wrapping the strip until it is too short.

5. Tuck the end into one of the folds. You may need to trim it slightly if it is a little too long.

6. Gently press the flat edges of the pentagon inward; this will cause the star to "inflate." Do the same with the last edge.

THE STARS ARE COUNTLESS AND DIVERSE. JUST LIKE YOUR FAILURES.

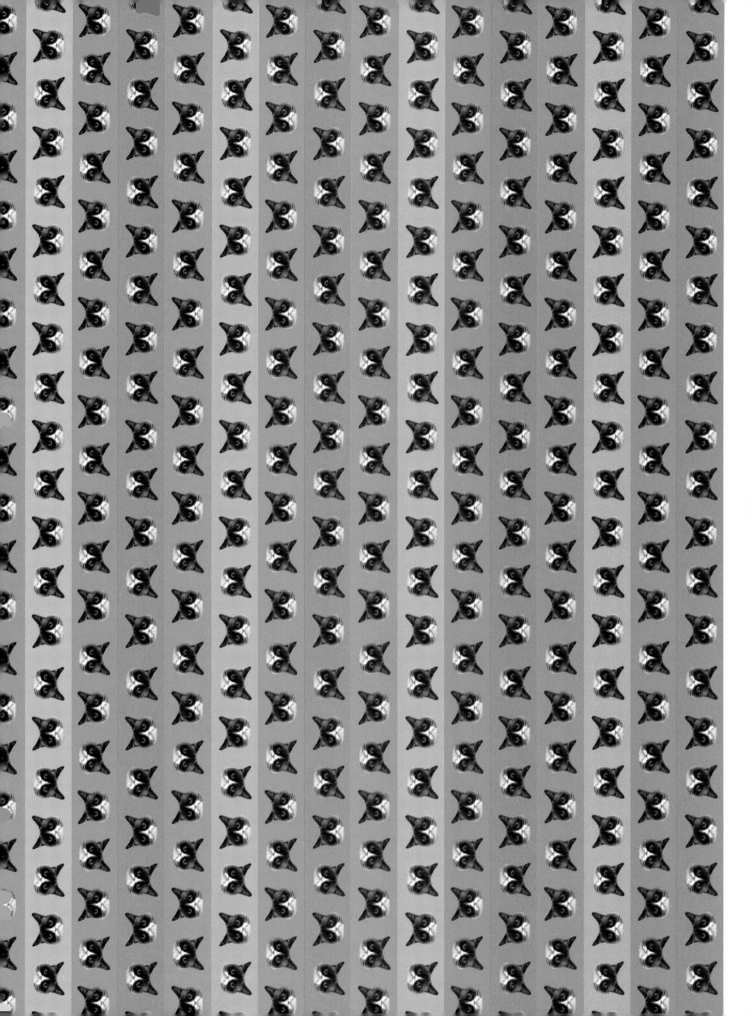

GRUMPY CAT DOESN'T LIKE | THROWING STARS

1. Fold in half vertically to create a crease. Unfold, then fold the left and right sides to the center crease.

2. Fold in half vertically so the fold is on the right and the Grumpy design is facing down.

3. Fold the top corner down and the bottom corner up.

4. Fold the top portion down , and the bottom potion up as shown.

5. Arrange the pieces as displayed, with the blue piece design side down and the orange piece design side up.

6. Fold the top blue corner down and tuck it beneath the orange flap. Repeat with the bottom blue flap.

7. Flip over. As in the last step, tuck the orange corners into the blue flaps.

8. You are now a grumpy ninja!

HOW ABOUT YOU PRACTICE BEING A NINJA AND DISAPPEAR.

THAT WOULD BE GREAT.

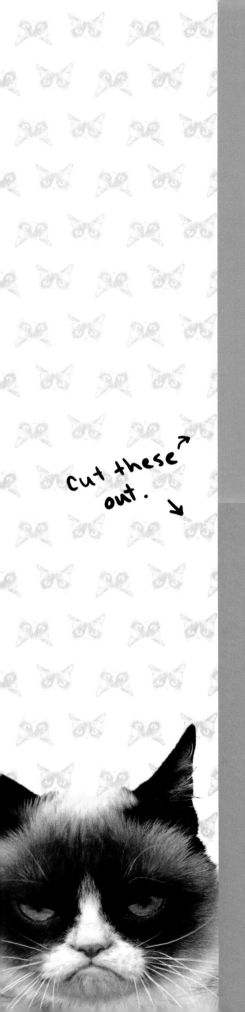

Cut these →
out.
↓

GRUMPY CAT DOESN'T LIKE PLACE CARDS

SCISSORS

THIS IS THE WORST SEAT.
THEY MUST REALLY NOT LIKE YOU.

THIS PARTY IS ALMOST AS
DULL AS YOU... ALMOST.

OH. THEY INVITED YOU?
GREAT.

NO ONE WANTS TO SIT
NEXT TO YOU.

THIS PARTY
SOUNDS LAME.

I'M LEAVING BEFORE THE
LAMENESS SPREADS.

1. Cut out each place card.

2. Carefully cut along the pale
solid line around Grumpy's ea

3. Fold each card in half.

4. Throw a grumpy dinner party

GRUMPY CAT DOESN'T LIKE BOOKMARKS

SCISSORS · EXACTO

1. Cut out the grumpy heads.

2. Use an exacto to carefully slice along the dotted lines (starting just below the ears).

3. Slide onto your page to save your place so you don't forget it. Like an idiot.

WOW.
YOU MUST BE
SUPER FORGETFUL.

I'M NOT
SURPRISED.